W9-BLG-728

DATE DUE

JAN 2 1 2011	
JAN 2 8 2011	
SEP 2 3 2015	

THE NHL: HISTORY AND HEROES

DETROIT RED WINGS

Published by Creative Education
P.O. Box 227, Mankato, Minnesota 56002
Creative Education is an imprint of The Creative Company.

DESIGN AND PRODUCTION BY **ZENO DESIGN**

Printed in the United States of America

PHOTOGRAPHS BY Corbis (Bettmann), Getty Images (Claus Anderson, Bruce Bennett
Studios, Eddie Hironaka, Robert Laberge/Allsport, Brian Miller/NHLI, Tom Pidgeon/Allsport,
Tom Pidgeon/NHLI, Dave Sandford, Dave Sandford/NHLI, Jamie Sabau/NHLI, Joseph
Scherschel//Time Life Pictures, Rick Stweart/Allsport, Ken Straiton), Hockey Hall of Fame
(Imperial Oil-Turofsky)

LIBRARY OF CONGRESS CATALOGING-IN-PUBLICATION DATA

Goodman, Michael E.
The story of the Detroit Red Wings / by Michael E. Goodman.
p. cm. — (The NHL: history and heroes)
Includes index
ISBN 978-1-58341-617-4
1. Detroit Red Wings (Hockey team)—History—Juvenile Literature. I. Title.

GV848.D47G665 2008
796.96'2640977434—dc22   2007015000

First Edition

9 8 7 6 5 4 3 2 1

COVER: Defenseman Nicklas Lidstrom

MICHAEL E. GOODIAN

THE NHL: HISTORY AND HEROES

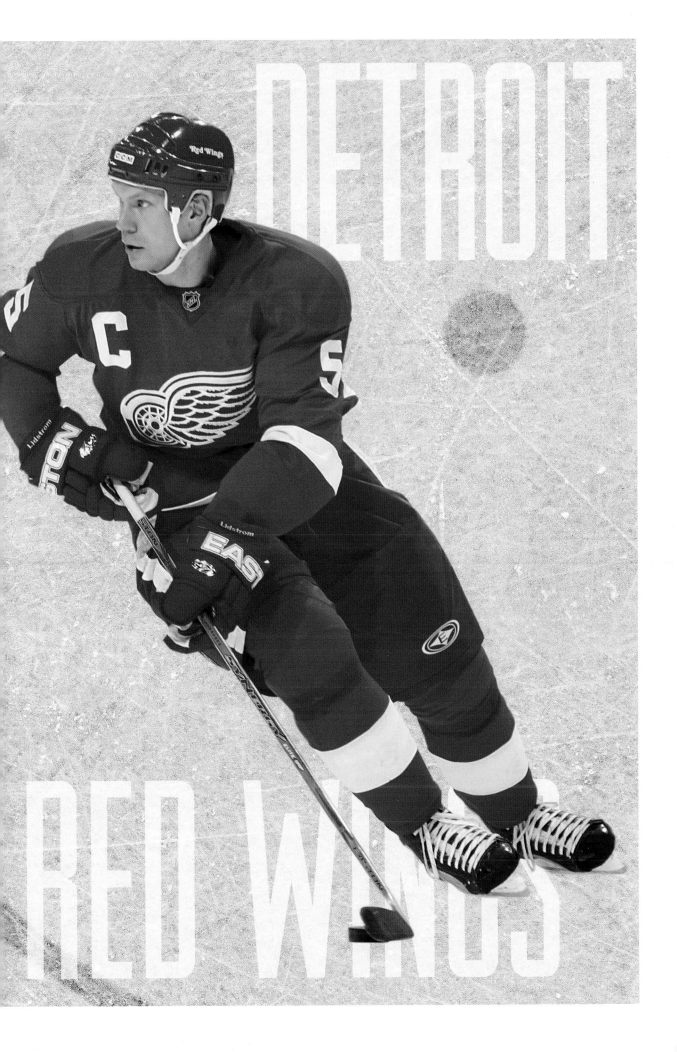

DETROIT

RED WINGS

AN AIR OF ANTICIPATION FILLED DETROIT'S JOE LOUIS ARENA ON JUNE 7, 1997. ROWDY DETROIT HOCKEY FANS PACKED THE BUILDING, HOPING TO SEE THEIR RED WINGS END A 42-YEAR STANLEY CUP DROUGHT. THE WINGS NEEDED JUST ONE MORE WIN OVER THE PHILADELPHIA FLYERS TO CAPTURE THEIR FIRST NATIONAL HOCKEY LEAGUE CHAMPIONSHIP SINCE 1955. THE ARENA STARTED ROCKING WHEN THE WINGS TOOK THE EARLY LEAD ON A HARD 55-FOOT (17 M) SLAP SHOT BY DEFENSEMAN NICKLAS LIDSTROM. THE ROAR CONTINUED TO BUILD

RED WINGS

AFTER A SECOND-PERIOD DETROIT GOAL. THEN THE PLACE BECAME PANDEMONIUM AS THE FINAL SECONDS TICKED OFF, AND A WILD VICTORY CELEBRATION BEGAN. "I'M GLAD THE GAME IS OVER," SAID RED WINGS TEAM CAPTAIN STEVE YZERMAN, "BUT I WISH IT HAD NEVER ENDED. SINCE I WAS FIVE YEARS OLD, I'VE WATCHED STANLEY CUP CELEBRATIONS AND DREAMED OF THE DAY THAT MAYBE I WOULD GET THERE." FOR YZERMAN AND DETROIT FANS, THAT DAY HAD COME AT LAST.

THE WINGS TAKE FLIGHT

IN 1701, A FRENCH COLONIST NAMED Antoine de la Mothe Cadillac established a military settlement between Lake Erie and Lake Huron and named it Fort Pontchartrain du Detroit. The fort was ceded to the British during the French and Indian War, and its name was shortened to Detroit. Noted for its hardworking residents, Detroit became an important industrial and commercial center in the 1800s and the hub of automobile manufacture in the United States in the early 1900s.

Detroit also became home to several successful professional sports franchises in the 1900s, starting with the Detroit Tigers baseball team and a football club named the Lions. In 1926, the city was also granted an expansion franchise in the National Hockey League (NHL). The team started out as the

Known for its long winters and large population of sports fans, Detroit has long been regarded as one of the world's great hockey cities.

8

Detroit Cougars and experienced several seasons of growing pains playing in the new Olympia Stadium. The club's fortunes began to brighten in 1932 when new owner James "Pop" Norris took over and started making key changes. Norris had once played for a Montreal amateur team called the Winged Wheelers, and he decided to adopt a winged wheel as the logo for his new club and to call it the Red Wings. Norris felt the name and logo were appropriate for a city known for its car manufacturing and fit the club's fast-moving style.

The club that Norris bought in 1932 already had an outstanding coach and general manager in place: Jack Adams. A former NHL player, Adams had been in Detroit since the Cougars' 1927–28 season and had begun building a winning tradition that would remain intact throughout his 36 years with the club. The demanding coach was known for driving his players hard. "There were no cliques on the Red Wings like on other teams," said Carl Liscombe, a star winger in the early 1940s. "We were united because we all hated Jack."

Steve Yzerman CENTER

When Steve Yzerman joined the Red Wings, the team was at a low point in its history. Quickly demonstrating both talent and leadership, Yzerman was named team captain at age 21. He proudly wore a "C" on his sweater for 20 seasons, the longest tenure as captain in NHL history. Yzerman began as a big scorer, topping the 50-goal mark five times. Then, under coach Scotty Bowman, Yzerman changed his game to become more defensive-minded, and the Wings soared in the standings. Said Detroit general manager Ken Holland, "He gave our organization a lot of hope and fulfilled it beyond anybody's wildest expectations."

RED WINGS SEASONS: 1983–2006
HEIGHT: 5-11 (180 cm)
WEIGHT: 185 (84 kg)

- 692 career goals
- 1,063 career assists
- 10-time All-Star
- 1998 Conn Smythe Trophy winner (as playoffs MVP)

Loud and demanding coach Jack Adams was so successful that the NHL named its Coach of the Year honor after him—the Jack Adams Award.

Still, the players worked hard for Adams, and he helped turn them into champions. During his 36-year tenure, the Red Wings would make the NHL playoffs 29 times, win 12 regular-season league championships (determined by the league's best record), and capture the Stanley Cup as world champions seven times. They would also feature some of the most exciting players in hockey. Because of this amazing success, fans throughout North America soon began calling Detroit "Hockeytown."

By the mid-1930s, the Red Wings were the league's top powerhouse, reaching the Stanley Cup Finals in 1934 and winning the Cup in both 1936 and 1937. Stars on those early Wings clubs included high-scoring wing Larry Aurie, bruising defenseman "Black Jack" Stewart, and stingy goaltender Normie Smith. Adams's team won a third Stanley Cup in 1943, sweeping the mighty Boston Bruins in the finals. But the Red Wings were only getting started. Even better years were just ahead, ushered in by the 1946 arrival of "Mr. Hockey."

"The Olympia was a beautiful place with a lot of noise. It's hard to describe how good the Olympia was. The ice was good, and the fans were right on top of you."

DETROIT WING PAUL WOODS ON OLYMPIA STADIUM

10

RED WINGS

Normie Smith's Revenge

WHEN THE RED WINGS TOOK ON THE Montreal Maroons in the first game of the 1936 playoffs, Detroit goalie Normie Smith had a special motivation to play his best. Smith had started his career with the Maroons, but they had given up on him. He found new life in Detroit and was determined to show his former employers that they had been wrong. As the game went on, the Maroons peppered Smith's goal with shot after shot, and he turned them all away. But the Wings were having their own problems scoring against Montreal's Lorne Chabot, and, after 60 minutes of play, the score remained 0–0. The two teams headed into overtime—in fact, into six overtimes. The game, which began at 8:30 P.M., didn't end until 2:25 A.M., when Detroit winger Mud Bruneteau scored the game's only goal. Smith had stopped 89 shots in shutting out the Maroons for a record 176 minutes. He blanked the Maroons again to win Game 2, and then allowed only one goal in Game 3 as Detroit completed a three-game sweep. Smith continued his goaltending mastery in the Stanley Cup Finals against the Toronto Maple Leafs, helping Detroit win its first NHL championship.

HOWE REIGNS IN HOCKEYTOWN

RIGHT WING GORDIE HOWE WOULD STAR for 25 seasons in Detroit, but he almost didn't put on a Red Wings sweater at all. When he was just 15, Howe, an outstanding amateur prospect from tiny Floral, Saskatchewan, had a tryout with the New York Rangers. Away from home for the first time in his life, he began to feel homesick and left the tryout early. The next year, he made another trip south, this time to audition for the Red Wings, who quickly signed him to a contract. Following a season in the minors, Howe arrived in the "Motor City" to stay before the 1946–47 season.

The young winger quickly proved that he had both talent and a mean streak. Standing 6 feet (183 cm) tall and weighing 205 pounds (93 kg), Howe was an imposing figure on the ice, and his physical

Although known for his gentlemanly behavior off the ice, Gordie Howe was a terror on it, pairing uncommon strength with rare scoring ability.

presence and temper earned him both fear and respect. If he felt an opponent had trespassed too far into his territory or taken a cheap shot at a teammate, Howe doled out retribution swiftly with a sharp elbow. He quickly became a favorite among Detroit fans, who dubbed him "Mr. Hockey." Howe would star with the Red Wings from 1946 to 1971, then play an additional seven years in both the World Hockey Association and the NHL. When he finally finished his career at age 52, Howe would tell sportswriters, "Say 'retired,' not 'quit.' I don't like the word 'quit.'"

Howe's resilient attitude was severely tested in the 1950 playoffs, when he was slammed into the boards while attempting to check Toronto Maple Leafs center Ted Kennedy. Howe suffered a life-threatening head injury, and doctors wondered if he would ever play again. Howe never had any doubts, though. He was back in the lineup at the start of the next season and won his first

Ted Lindsay WING

Sometimes known as "Terrible-Tempered Ted" because of his flying fists and sharp tongue, Ted Lindsay was a key member of Detroit's "Production Line," helping the Red Wings win four Stanley Cups in the 1940s and '50s. Coach Jack Adams named Lindsay team captain in 1953, declaring, "He is a player who never quits himself and can stir his team up in the dressing room and on the ice." Lindsay was also an activist off the ice, helping to form the first NHL players' union in 1957 and even boycotting his Hall of Fame induction because his wife and other women could not attend.

RED WINGS SEASONS: 1944–57, 1964–65
HEIGHT: 5-8 (173 cm)
WEIGHT: 160 (73 kg)

- 379 career goals
- 472 career assists
- 10-time All-Star
- Hockey Hall of Fame inductee (1966)

Aggressive play made Ted Lindsay (right) seem bigger than 5-foot-8 (173 cm) and win the 1950 Art Ross Trophy as the NHL's leading scorer.

league scoring title that year. Before he retired, Howe would win five more scoring titles and six Hart Trophies as the NHL's Most Valuable Player (MVP).

"I still believe that the five Stanley Cups that Montreal won [from 1956 to 1960] should have been ours. At worst we should have won three of the five. We had the team. We had the talent. We had the chemistry."

DETROIT DEFENSEMAN TED LINDSAY

With Howe as the cornerstone, Jack Adams—who had stepped down as coach but was still serving as general manager—built a sports dynasty in the late 1940s and early '50s. Beginning in 1948–49, the Red Wings finished with the best regular-season record in the NHL for seven straight years and captured four Stanley Cups. Detroit's famed "Production Line" of Howe at right wing, Sid Abel at center, and Ted Lindsay at left wing was a lethal offensive machine. "They could score goals in their sleep," Adams said.

During the 1949–50 season, Lindsay, Abel, and Howe finished 1-2-3 respectively in the NHL scoring race as the Wings soared to a second straight regular-season title. Detroit faced a tough challenge in the playoffs after Howe went down, but the club battled back to reach the Stanley Cup Finals against the New York Rangers and then captured the Cup in the deciding Game 7 on a double-overtime goal by reserve wing Pete Babando.

The Red Wings were flying high, but Adams decided to make a key change before the 1950–51 season, bringing up 20-year-old rookie Terry Sawchuk

Eight Legs, One New Tradition

ON THE NIGHT OF APRIL 15, 1952, brothers Pete and Jerry Cusimano, who owned a Detroit fish market, brought an unusual good luck charm to Olympia Stadium for Game 4 of the Stanley Cup Finals between Detroit and Toronto—a dead octopus. The Wings had already won seven playoff games in the semifinals and Finals and needed just one more victory to capture the Cup. The Cusimanos figured that tossing an eight-legged cephalopod onto the ice before the game would assure an eighth victory for their home team. The Olympia maintenance crew wasn't too happy when the octopus splattered onto the ice, but the fans went crazy. And the Wings won the game handily, 3–0. A new tradition was born, as Detroit fans began throwing out octopi after Red Wings players scored goals during home playoff games in later years. Team management tried to outlaw the practice, but Detroit fans still found ways to sneak the octopi into the arena. Fans set an unofficial record by heaving 54 octopi onto the ice at Joe Louis Arena during Game 2 of the 1993 Stanley Cup Finals. Today, a 30-foot (9 m) purple styrofoam octopus hangs above the arena, bringing luck to the Wings.

from the minor leagues to take over in goal. The move had spectacular results. Sawchuk led the league with 11 shutouts in 1950–51 and helped the Wings win three Stanley Cups in the four seasons between 1952 and 1955. One opposing coach commented, "We're watching hockey's greatest goalie, and I'm sure we'll still be saying that about Sawchuk years from now."

Although the Production Line and Sawchuk got most of the headlines, the Red Wings teams of the 1950s also featured defenseman Red Kelly, a nine-time All-Star, and center Alex Delvecchio, a three-time winner of the Lady Byng Trophy for sportsmanship. Delvecchio played in Detroit for 24 seasons, but his greatest moments came early in his career during Game 7 of the 1955 Stanley Cup Finals against the Montreal Canadiens. In that game, he scored two spectacular goals—one on an end-to-end solo rush down the ice—that propelled Detroit to a 3–1 victory and the seventh Stanley Cup in club history.

Gordie Howe WING

During the 1950s, the biggest argument among hockey fans involved who was a better all-around player—Gordie Howe or Maurice "Rocket" Richard of the Montreal Canadiens. When Richard retired, he settled the argument: "Gordie was better. He could do everything." Howe finished in the top five in NHL scoring for 20 consecutive seasons, but his value on the ice extended well beyond goals. Big and powerful, he was never reluctant to use his elbows to intimidate opponents. "I'm not dirty," he once said. "I'd rather say 'aggressive.'" For his skills as both a scorer and an intimidator, Howe earned the nickname "Mr. Hockey."

RED WINGS SEASONS: 1946–71
HEIGHT: 6-0 (183 cm)
WEIGHT: 205 (93 kg)

- 801 career goals
- 1,767 career games (most all-time)
- 6-time Hart Trophy winner (as league MVP)
- Hockey Hall of Fame inductee (1972)

Terry Sawchuk suffered numerous injuries in the 1950s but still played every game like it was his last, becoming an 11-time All-Star in the process.

THE LONG DROUGHT BEGINS

THE 1955 CUP TRIUMPH MARKED THE END of the Red Wings' golden era. It would be more than four decades before the Stanley Cup would return to Detroit. The Red Wings came close many times, particularly in the early 1960s. Led by Howe and center Norm Ullman, the Wings reached the Stanley Cup Finals four times in the '60s, only to come in second each year. Then, NHL expansion began to change the sport's landscape, as the six-team league doubled in size in 1967 and added more new teams every few years after that. Talent became spread out through the league, and the Red Wings fell behind younger clubs in the standings. The team made the playoffs only once between 1967 and 1977, and fans began calling their aging stars the "Gray Wings."

Speedy newcomer Marcel Dionne gave Red Wings fans something to cheer about in 1971–72, scoring an NHL rookie–record 77 points.

Still, Detroit fans found reasons to cheer during the 1970s. In 1972-73, winger Mickey Redmond became the first Red Wings player to score 50 goals in a season—a feat he repeated the next season. Fellow wing Danny Grant became the team's second 50-goal man in 1974-75. But the best Detroit player of that era was dynamic center Marcel Dionne, a pint-sized French-Canadian who was the Wings' top pick in the 1971 NHL Draft. Setting team records for assists and points (goals plus assists), Dionne quickly established himself as one of the league's elite players.

"Players wanted to be traded to the Red Wings. They had Gordie Howe. They had good defense and goaltending. But it wasn't just the talent. The Red Wings were just better organized than other NHL teams."

DETROIT DEFENSEMAN BILL GADSBY

However, after four non-playoff seasons with the Red Wings, Dionne signed with the Los Angeles Kings, leaving Detroit without a leader. "Things were just too chaotic [in Detroit]," Dionne explained. "Coaches, management, and so many players were coming in and going out." Even the Red Wings' ownership changed. In June 1982, Little Caesars pizza millionaires Mike and Marian Ilitch bought the team. The Ilitches poured money into rebuilding the club, and huge crowds began to pack Joe Louis Arena for every Wings game, cheering as their team began a slow return to the top.

A Doubly Special Night

ON NOVEMBER 10, 1963, DETROIT HOCKEY fans packed Olympia Stadium, hoping to see one of hockey's most cherished records broken. In fact, they witnessed two record performances. Coming into the game against the Montreal Canadiens, Gordie Howe had scored 544 goals in his career, the same total as retired Montreal winger Maurice "Rocket" Richard. Howe needed to "light the lamp" just one more time to become the all-time scoring leader. Late in the second period, Howe slammed the puck past Montreal goalie Charlie Hodge for the record-breaker, and the fans gave him a 15-minute standing ovation. When the fans resumed their seats, they realized that they had something else special to cheer for that evening. While Howe had established himself as the NHL's greatest at putting the puck in the net, Red Wings goalie Terry Sawchuk was set to tie the record for keeping the puck out of the net. If Sawchuk could hold Montreal scoreless in the third period, he would match former Montreal goaltender George Hainesworth's total of 94 career shutouts. To the fans' delight, Sawchuk turned away all 13 shots he faced in the last period to notch number 94. He would break the record two months later in another game against Montreal.

One of the Ilitches' first moves was to lure Jimmy Devellano away from the reigning world champion New York Islanders to become Detroit's general manager. Devellano's first move was to select Steve Yzerman, an 18-year-old center from Ottawa, with the fourth overall pick in the 1983 NHL Draft. "Steve Yzerman will be the cornerstone of this team for many years to come," Devellano accurately predicted.

Yzerman set team rookie records with 39 goals and 87 points (goals plus assists) in 1983–84 to help the Red Wings reach the playoffs for the first time in six years. Then, beginning in 1987–88, he scored 100-plus points in six consecutive seasons to lead the club back to its familiar position among the NHL's elite. Only 21 years old when he was named team captain in 1986, the soft-spoken Yzerman led by example rather than emotion. "People sometimes look for the rah-rah stuff ... but that's not what makes someone a leader,"

Jack Stewart DEFENSEMAN

Tough and tenacious, Jack Stewart perfected the art of body checking on defense. He earned the nickname "Black Jack" because opponents said that he seemed to be carrying a blackjack when he smashed into them at the blue line. As one Detroit sportswriter noted, "It was almost impossible getting past him without paying a price. He had a way of putting his full body into a check, and the impact could be felt throughout the arena." Stewart was an All-Star in 3 of his 12 seasons in the league and, despite scoring few goals, earned a place in the Hockey Hall of Fame.

RED WINGS SEASONS: 1938–43, 1945–50
HEIGHT: 5-11 (180 cm)
WEIGHT: 180 (82 kg)

- 31 career goals
- 1945–46 NHL leader in penalty minutes
- 3-time All-Star
- Hockey Hall of Fame inductee (1964)

The quiet leadership and clutch scoring of "The Captain," longtime star Steve Yzerman, helped carry the Red Wings to three Stanley Cup titles.

Yzerman said. "It's about the willingness to pay the price, to compete harder

than the other guys."

Yzerman and two former European standouts, winger Petr Klima from

Czechoslovakia and center Sergei Fedorov from the former Soviet Union, helped

the Red Wings become the second-best team in the NHL. Unfortunately, the

league's best team—the Edmonton Oilers—played in the same conference.

Detroit reached the Campbell Conference Finals in both 1987 and 1988 but was

eliminated each year by Edmonton and its star center, Wayne Gretzky. For the

proud Detroit franchise, the long Stanley Cup drought was exasperating. The

team had come so far, but its turnaround would not be complete until the

Cup returned to Hockeytown.

"We were a muck-and-grind team. We
played better defense than most teams,
and we scored timely goals. We were also
a very tough team."

DETROIT GOALTENDER GREG STEFAN
ON THE 1980S RED WINGS

Sergei Fedorov established himself as one of the most versatile NHL players of the 1990s, a scoring machine who could play fierce defense.

A CUP AT LAST

IN THE SUMMER OF 1993, FOLLOWING ANOTHER tough playoff loss, Mike Ilitch hired Scotty Bowman, the NHL's all-time winningest coach, to guide the Red Wings. Bowman already possessed six championship rings, and Ilitch believed he could have the same winning touch in Detroit. "Now is the time to win the Stanley Cup," the owner said the day he hired Bowman. "You've got to go with winners. Now, I like my chances."

Bowman quickly began remolding the club to fit the system he believed in. The Wings were the most potent offensive team in the NHL, but Bowman asked his players to think defense first. He brought in veteran goalie Mike Vernon to share time with young

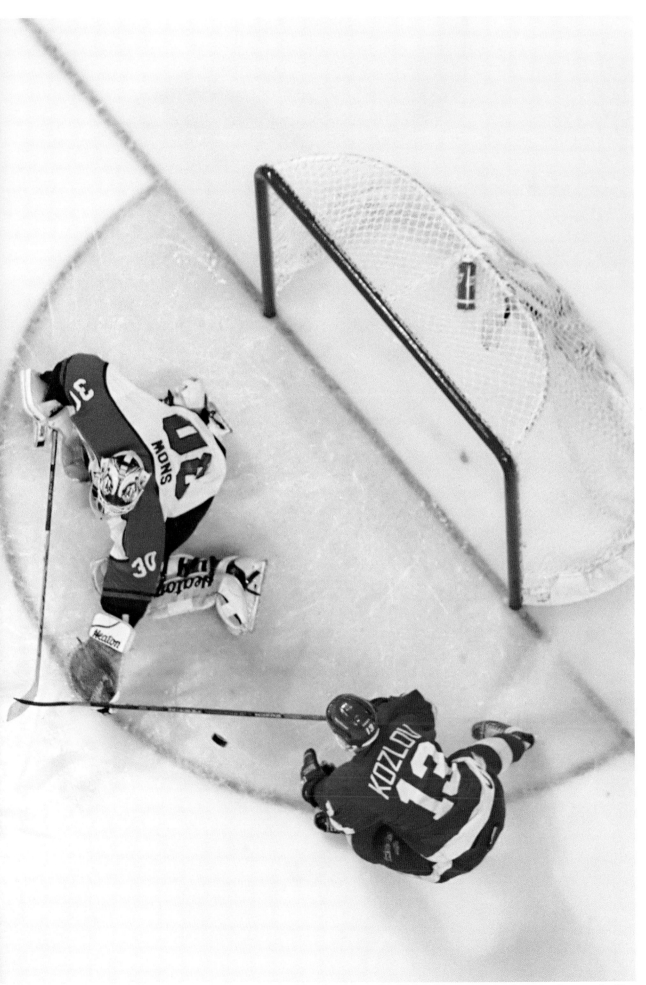

During his eight seasons in a Red Wings sweater, Slava Kozlov bewildered many a goalie with his slick moves on breakaway scoring opportunities.

star Chris Osgood and gave defensemen Paul Coffey and Vladimir Konstantinov more responsibility on the ice. The offense remained powerful, too, thanks to Yzerman, Fedorov, center/wing Keith Primeau, and center Slava Kozlov. In Bowman's second season at the helm (1994–95), the Red Wings earned the Presidents' Trophy with the best regular-season record in the NHL and reached the Stanley Cup Finals for the first time in 29 years. Then they were embarrassed as the tight-checking New Jersey Devils swept them in the Finals in four games. "We never really got frustrated during the series," Steve Yzerman said. "It didn't go long enough for us to get frustrated."

The Wings bounced back the next season to set an NHL record with 62 victories, only to fall to the Colorado Avalanche in a fight-filled Western Conference Finals series. There was no denying the Wings in 1996–97, however, thanks in large part to two significant events during the season. The first came in early

Red Kelly DEFENSEMAN

While Jack Stewart was known for his aggressiveness on the ice, Leonard "Red" Kelly was considered one of the game's great gentlemen. Four times, he was awarded the Lady Byng Trophy for outstanding sportsmanship. Kelly was both talented and versatile. After starring on defense for the Red Wings for 13 seasons, he became an All-Star center for the Toronto Maple Leafs for the rest of his career. A welterweight boxer as a youth, Kelly was an effective checker, but he tended to use speed and finesse more than brawn. During his hockey career, he also served as a member of the Canadian parliament.

RED WINGS SEASONS: 1947–60
HEIGHT: 6-0 (183 cm)
WEIGHT: 195 (88 kg)

- 281 career goals
- 542 career assists
- 4-time Lady Byng Trophy winner
- Hockey Hall of Fame inductee (1969)

A three-time All-Star (1996, 1997, and 1998), netminder Chris Osgood spent eight years in Detroit in the '90s, then returned for a second stint in 2005.

October, when the Wings traded with the Hartford Whalers to obtain All-Star winger Brendan Shanahan. Big (6-foot-3 [185 cm] and 220 pounds [100 kg]) and talented, Shanahan would lead the team in goals and points. "I'm not saying I'm the missing piece of the puzzle," Shanahan announced upon arriving in Detroit, "but I definitely think I can be a big piece of that puzzle."

The second key event took place during a late-season game against Colorado. The Red Wings had held a grudge against the Avalanche for nearly a year, ever since Colorado wing Claude Lemieux had blindsided Detroit center Kris Draper during the 1996 playoffs. The incident had put Draper out of commission for the series and was a big factor in the Wings' playoff elimination. In late March 1997, the two teams met in Detroit. Both teams ranked near the top of the Western Conference standings and would likely face each other in the playoffs again. Emotions were high that night, and a brawl broke out in which Red Wings winger Darren McCarty pummeled Lemieux and earned some revenge for his team. The fight seemed to galvanize the Wings; they captured that contest on a McCarty goal in overtime and kept winning right into the playoffs. "Detroit won the Stanley Cup that night," Colorado goalie Patrick Roy remarked after the playoffs. In the postseason, the Wings, led by Vernon's hot goaltending, quickly disposed of the St. Louis Blues, Mighty Ducks of Anaheim, and Colorado to earn a berth in the Stanley Cup Finals against the favored Philadelphia Flyers.

Tough wing Darren McCarty assumed the role of enforcer for Detroit in the late '90s, playing some of his best games against rival Colorado.

Then, just as they had been upset in a four-game sweep in 1995, the Red Wings routed the Flyers in four straight contests. For the first time in 42 years, the Stanley Cup had come home to Detroit. For Steve Yzerman, skating around the ice in Joe Louis Arena holding the giant trophy over his head was a lifelong dream from which he didn't want to wake up. "I wanted the game back, so I could watch the whole thing again and never forget a minute of it," he said.

"When people ask me what it was like to play 10 years in Detroit, I always say it was great because we were winning every year."

DETROIT WING MARTY PAVELICH

Tempering Joy with Sadness

THE SPIRITS OF RED WINGS PLAYERS and their fans were soaring following the team's long-awaited Stanley Cup victory in 1997, but no one celebrated for very long. Only six days after the championship game, star defenseman Vladimir Konstantinov—an aggressive defender and fan favorite—and team masseur Sergei Mnatsakanov were critically injured in a limousine crash that ended their careers. The entire franchise was devastated, and the accident weighed heavily on the minds of all the Red Wings players. The players decided to dedicate the following season to Konstantinov and resolved to win a second championship in his honor. During the 1998 playoffs, the Wings defeated the Phoenix Coyotes, St. Louis Blues, and Dallas Stars in the first three rounds and then swept the Washington Capitals in the Stanley Cup Finals. In an emotional postgame celebration, Konstantinov came onto the ice in his wheelchair to join the team. Steve Yzerman placed the Stanley Cup in his hands as his teammates pushed the chair around the arena in a victory lap. Fans in Detroit and all over North America were touched by the celebration, and reporters around the world wrote that no team had ever deserved to repeat as champions as much as these Red Wings.

STAYING ON TOP

THE WINGS SUCCESSFULLY DEFENDED THEIR title the next season, keeping the Cup in Hockeytown for another year, and Yzerman won the Conn Smythe Trophy as the playoffs MVP. Detroit reached the playoffs the next two seasons as well but was stopped both times in the second round by rival Colorado and its All-Star goaltender, Patrick Roy.

After his club was ousted in the first round by the Los Angeles Kings in 2001, Bowman decided it was time to shake things up in Detroit. He added three future Hall-of-Famers—goalie Dominik Hasek and wingers Luc Robitaille and Brett Hull—to his already star-studded lineup. The moves paid off as the Red Wings won the Presidents' Trophy during the regular

Brett Hull was 36 years old when he joined Detroit in 2001 but was still a dangerous scorer, averaging 31 goals a year the next three seasons.

season and then raced to their third Cup triumph in six years. While the new-comers all played roles in the Stanley Cup victory, the real star was veteran defenseman Nicklas Lidstrom, who had been anchoring the club's defense for more than a decade. The Swedish backliner tallied five goals during the playoffs, including one game winner, and became the first European-born player to win the Conn Smythe Trophy.

After establishing an NHL coaching record with his ninth Stanley Cup tri-umph, Bowman stepped down and passed the team's coaching reins to his longtime assistant, Dave Lewis. The Wings continued to excel in the regular season the next two years under Lewis but came up short in the playoffs. So Detroit management turned to Mike Babcock to take over before the 2005–06 season. Babcock had previously taken a young Mighty Ducks of Anaheim fran-chise all the way to the Stanley Cup Finals and had coached the Canadian national team to a gold medal in the 2004 World Hockey Championship. He brought to Detroit a reputation as a no-nonsense coach. "There are no shortcuts with him," said Detroit executive Jim Nill. "He's a career hockey guy, he's very well prepared, and he's very intense. He demands a lot and has high standards."

Babcock quickly assessed his new team to determine how best to maxi-mize its talent. He decided to put extra responsibility on his veteran defenders, Lidstrom and Chris Chelios, and to focus on developing the club's two young offensive stars, center Pavel Datsyuk of Russia and wing Henrik Zetterberg of

Hall of Fame South

THE HOCKEY HALL OF FAME MAY BE LOCATED in Toronto, Ontario, but during the 2001–02 season, a new wing seemed to open in Detroit. That year, Scotty Bowman, who was already in the Hall himself, put together a team that featured at least nine future Hall of Fame members and led them to a Stanley Cup. Before the season, general manager Ken Holland engineered deals to bring in All-Star forwards Brett Hull and Luc Robitaille and goalie Dominick Hasek. The big question was whether the new arrivals could blend in smoothly with the future Hall-of-Famers who were already playing in Detroit—centers Steve Yzerman, Sergei Fedorov, and Igor Larionov, left wing Brendan Shanahan, and defensemen Nicklas Lidstrom and Chris Chelios. The answer came quickly. The club raced out to a terrific start, winning 15 and tying 3 of its first 25 games, and breezed to the best record in the league. It was a year of milestones for several future Hall members, as Yzerman recorded his 1,000th assist, Robitaille notched his 600th goal, and Shanahan tallied his 500th goal and 1,000th point. Despite all of its talent, the team struggled early in the playoffs before eventually winning the franchise's 10th Stanley Cup.

Sweden. Although they grew up speaking different languages, the two forwards had a special bond on the ice. "We understand each other so well," said Datsyuk. "We speak in a hockey language."

While Detroit fans were excited about their new coach and young stars, they were also saddened when Steve Yzerman decided to retire in the summer of 2006. "The Captain" had been the heart of the team for 22 seasons, and a packed house turned out in Joe Louis Arena on January 2, 2007, to cheer as his number 19 sweater was retired and raised to the rafters alongside those of such former Red Wings greats as Gordie Howe, Alex Delvecchio, and Ted Lindsay. Yzerman's capital "C" was passed on to Nicklas Lidstrom, who pledged to carry on the winning tradition that Yzerman had helped foster.

While Yzerman rode off into the sunset, Coach Babcock's plan played out flawlessly in 2007–08, as the veteran Red Wings rolled to a terrific 54–21–7

RED WINGS ALL-TIME TEAM

Terry Sawchuk GOALIE

As a rookie in 1950–51, Terry Sawchuk surprised hockey experts by recording a league-leading 11 shutouts. The next year, he was even better, notching 12 shutouts and winning his first Vezina Trophy as the NHL's top goaltender. Sawchuk was one of the first goalies of his time to crouch in front of the net rather than stand up straight. "It gave me better balance," he explained, "and helped me keep better track of the puck through the players' legs on screened shots." Crouching also put Sawchuk more in the line of fire, especially since he didn't wear a mask for most of his career.

RED WINGS SEASONS: 1949–55, 1957–64, 1968–69
HEIGHT: 5–11 (180 cm)
WEIGHT: 190 (86 kg)

• 447 career wins
• 103 career shutouts (most all-time)
• 4-time Vezina Trophy winner (as best goaltender)
• Hockey Hall of Fame inductee (1971)

Pavel Datsyuk (right) scored often for the Red Wings and did so with class, winning the Lady Byng Trophy in both 2006 and 2007.

record. But in a first-round playoff matchup against the Nashville Predators, Hasek looked shaky in the goal. Babcock then made a risky move, benching the longtime star and inserting veteran backup Chris Osgood in his place.

The move paid off. With great goaltending from Osgood, a charged-up offense featuring Datsyuk and Zetterberg, and the defensive leadership of Lidstrom, Detroit powered past the Predators, Avalanche, and Dallas Stars to reach the Stanley Cup Finals. And although a young and talented Pittsburgh Penguins squad put up a fight, the Red Wings would not be denied, winning the championship four games to two. When the final horn sounded in Game 6, Lidstrom was the first man to lift the Stanley Cup over his head. "I've been over here [in the U.S.] for a long time, and I watched Steve Yzerman hoist it three times in the past," said the Swedish star. "I'm very proud of being a captain of the Red Wings."

The Detroit Red Wings and their fans have a special bond. For more than 80 years, the fans have packed Motor City arenas to proclaim their devotion (and toss an occasional octopus). And the Red Wings have entertained their fans season after season with a tough, hard-nosed style of play on the ice. Today's Wings promise to maintain that style and to help Detroit remain Hockeytown U.S.A. for many years to come.

"This organization—Hockeytown—was built by Howe, Delvecchio, Lindsay, Sawchuck, Abel.... The only way we can say thank you, to truly honor them, is to play hard and to play with pride to honor the logo."

DETROIT CENTER STEVE YZERMAN

Long-Term Commitments

WHEN STEVE YZERMAN ANNOUNCED HIS retirement in July 2006, it marked the end of a 22-season career in the Motor City. During that time, Yzerman led Detroit to three Stanley Cups and to playoff appearances in each of the last 15 years of his career. Only Gordie Howe holds as many franchise scoring records. In these days of rapid player movement in all professional sports, spending 22 years with the same team seems pretty remarkable. However, Yzerman's long stay is not so unusual among Red Wings greats. Howe spent his first 25 seasons playing for the Red Wings before coming out of retirement to play with his two sons in the World Hockey Association. Alex Delvecchio nearly matched Howe, playing 24 seasons and 1,550 games in a Red Wings sweater. And longtime coach and general manager Jack Adams served the franchise loyally for 36 years. How did these men put in such long-term commitments to the game and to the team? Howe summed it up: "You've got to love what you're doing. If you love it, you can overcome any handicap or the soreness or all the aches and pains, and continue to play for a long, long time."

The Red Wings featured a talented, veteran defense in the early 2000s, including skaters Nicklas Lidstrom and Chris Chelios and goalie Dominik Hasek.

Scotty Bowman COACH

No NHL coach may ever come close to matching Scotty Bowman's NHL records of 1,244 regular-season wins and 1,467 combined regular-season and playoff victories. Bowman arrived in Detroit in 1993 after having led the Montreal Canadiens and Pittsburgh Penguins to Stanley Cup titles. Then he enhanced his record with three more championships in Hockeytown. A demanding leader, Bowman insisted that his players buy in to his system of hard-nosed hockey or else leave his team. One writer noted that Bowman's players hated him for 364 days a year and liked him only on the day they picked up their Stanley Cup rings.

RED WINGS SEASONS AS COACH: 1993–2002
NHL COACHING RECORD: 1,244–583–314
STANLEY CUP CHAMPIONSHIPS WITH DETROIT: 1997, 1998, 2002
2-TIME NHL COACH OF THE YEAR

INDEX